SIGNPOSTS

SIGNPOSTS

David Patterson

XULON PRESS

Xulon Press
2301 Lucien Way #415
Maitland, FL 32751
407.339.4217
www.xulonpress.com

© 2023 by David Patterson

All rights reserved solely by the author. The author guarantees all contents are original and do not infringe upon the legal rights of any other person or work. No part of this book may be reproduced in any form without the permission of the author.

Due to the changing nature of the Internet, if there are any web addresses, links, or URLs included in this manuscript, these may have been altered and may no longer be accessible. The views and opinions shared in this book belong solely to the author and do not necessarily reflect those of the publisher. The publisher therefore disclaims responsibility for the views or opinions expressed within the work.

Unless otherwise indicated, Scripture quotations taken from the Holy Bible, New International Version (NIV). Copyright © 1973, 1978, 1984, 2011 by Biblica, Inc.™. Used by permission. All rights reserved.

Paperback ISBN-13: 978-1-66287-205-1
Ebook ISBN-13: 978-1-66287-206-8

Table of Contents

PREFACE ix

PART ONE: MY JOURNEY

Chapter 1: EDEN 3
Chapter 2: PRAYER 7
Chapter 3: ANGEL HAND 9
Chapter 4: RAGGEDY MAN 11
Chapter 5: WELL DONE, SOLDIER 15
Chapter 6: THE NUTCRACKER 19
Chapter 7: THE COFFEE SHOP 21
Chapter 8: MAKING THE NEWS 27
Chapter 9: A STRANGE ENCOUNTER 33
Chapter 10: THE OUTCASTS 37
Chapter 11: THE MISSION TRIP 41
Chapter 12: THE CUP OF COFFEE 45
Chapter 13: IT'S A WONDERFUL LIFE 47
Chapter 14: HOUSE MIRACLE 51
Chapter 15: THE HUMBLING 55
Chapter 16: DESIRES FULFILLED 57

PART TWO: YOUR JOURNEY

Chapter 17: ARE YOU ON THE JOURNEY? 63
Chapter 18: THE IMPORTANCE OF
              WATERSHED MOMENTS 65
Chapter 19: SOME TIPS FOR THE JOURNEY 67
Chapter 20: LEAVING A POSITIVE LEGACY 75
Chapter 21: ENDING THE JOURNEY WELL 79

POSTSCRIPT 83

PREFACE

WE ARE ALL familiar with the signposts along the roadside that show the way to where we are going. Without them, our journey would be much more difficult (Although I do recognize that GPS has enabled us to travel "blind" as never before). But the term is used in a broader, figurative sense to speak of "something that serves as a clue or indication" (The Free Dictionary)[1] or a "guide, beacon" (Merriam-Webster)[2]. For the Christian, there is (or should be) a recognition that God places spiritual signposts along the Christian journey to point us in the direction that God would have us go. Our ultimate source of direction and guidance, of course, is the Bible itself, but I have come to be convinced that God makes those biblical truths more real to us through key experiences in our lives. These experiences serve as turning points where God speaks and His direction for our lives becomes clearer than ever before. I have had many such "aha" moments in my life, and this book is my attempt to share some of those moments and to encourage the reader to look for such signposts in their own lives and find their meaning for themselves.

---

[1] American Heritage® Dictionary of the English Language, Fifth Edition. Copyright © 2016 by Houghton Mifflin Harcourt Publishing Company. Published by Houghton Mifflin Harcourt Publishing Company. All rights reserved.

[2] "Signpost." *Merriam-Webster.com Dictionary,* Merriam-Webster, https://www.merriam-webster.com/dictionary/signpost. Accessed 4 Jan. 2023.

SIGNPOSTS

Please understand that I do not share my own experiences to set myself up as the ultimate standard. I have often failed to fully live up to the lessons learned and perhaps would have seen more of these signposts along the way if I had always kept my spiritual eyes open. Nevertheless, I feel compelled to make known the way God has worked in my life and pass it on to others. I guess you could say that I am setting up my own signpost and hope it may help to make the journey more pleasant and productive for those who read my words.

PART ONE: MY JOURNEY

Chapter 1

EDEN

He has made everything beautiful in its time.
He has also set eternity in the hearts of men…
(Ecclesiastes 3:11 NIV)

I HAVE ALWAYS BEEN convinced that this verse in the Bible is telling us two important things. First, that everything that happens in life is in accordance with the higher purposes of God. And second, that every person is born with an inner longing for something greater, something "outer and other" and beyond this earthly life itself. Something permanent and unending. When I placed my faith in Christ at a young age, I realized that what my heart longed for was eternal life itself and that that life was received through Him; however, there was also a signpost that God gave me as a child growing up that pointed me to the reality of that truth in my own everyday experience.

The highlight of my summer every year was spending time on my grandparents' farm in Kansas. I can only characterize those days as times of absolute bliss. They were filled with family reunions, homemade ice cream and pie, seemingly unending fireworks on the Fourth of July, and constant fun with aunts, uncles, and cousins. My Grandpa Phelps was a godly man; I even remember him singing hymns as he worked. He took me along with him when hoeing weeds in the melon and cantaloupe patches and put up with the fact that I did little work and mostly watched for bugs and told him which ones I thought were good and which ones were bad. He would take us for tractor rides and show us how to fish with cane poles, using plain string with homemade hooks and earthworms freshly dug from the ground. His melons were huge and tasted better than anything I had eaten since. Grandma Phelps set up a playhouse for us kids in the backyard, furnishing it with an old kitchen stove, bookcase, picnic table, and wash basin equipped with a discarded hand-operated water pump. This served as the center of our childhood play. All of my siblings and cousins would mimic family life and I still remember playing the role of the son who was a soldier coming home from war. When nightfall came, there were frequent games of flashlight tag with unlimited places to hide at both my grandparents' farm and the adjacent farm of my great aunt and uncle.

Another feature of those times was the opportunity to go on country calls with my favorite uncle, who was a veterinarian. Uncle Glenn had a great sense of humor and made every trip a time of adventure and fun. His favorite trick was to get one of the cousins to get out of the truck to pick something up off of the side of the road and then drive off. He always came back, of course, but only after driving just fast enough to keep you from grabbing the door handle for quite a distance. He loved his work, and I admired his great skill at caring for animals and even considered one day becoming a veterinarian myself. Now that I think of it, shepherding people as a pastor is not that different in many ways, but that is getting ahead of the story.

Needless to say, I loved farm life and became a country boy at heart. Some other special memories I have include collecting chicken eggs from the chicken coop in the morning, chasing down the many farm cats used as mousers, listening to the mournful calls of the mourning doves in the hedge beyond the coop (I still think of the farm whenever I hear them), the sound of cicadas in the trees in the evenings (we called them locusts), the fireflies lighting up the night (we often caught some in a jar and they served as a night-light when we went to bed). I even loved the outhouse out back and the hand pumps we had to crank for water. My mom told me I was very angry when an electric pump was installed and provided running water for a newly remodeled, modern bathroom. For quite a while, I refused to use the bathroom and used the outhouse instead.

I could go on and on with many stories of those days, but let me get to the point. The farm was my paradise. It fed a longing in my heart, but it ultimately only pointed to something greater. As I grew older, I learned that life is difficult. Not exactly paradise. My grandpa passed away. The farm eventually had to be sold. I still remember lying in the tree house on the farm for the last time as a teenager, looking up at the sky and for the first time realizing that all of this was temporary and that the mosquitoes and flies I seemed to be able to ignore when I was younger now were a source of constant irritation. Playing in the playhouse was no longer fun. I was growing up and things were changing. Melancholy feelings replaced much of the joy, but I took with me something that could never be taken away. A taste of Eden. A glimpse of heaven. A signpost pointing to life beyond this life. To eternity itself.

Chapter 2

PRAYER

*And pray in the Spirit on all occasions
with all kinds of prayers and requests...
(Ephesians 6:18 NIV)*

WHILE AN UNMARRIED student in college, God began to take hold of my heart and for the first time, my spiritual life began to reflect a deep sensitivity to God's presence. The Christianity that I had been taught all my life by my parents and the church we attended had become more refined and deeply personal. God took this opportunity to speak to me in a way that was clear and undeniable.

While studying in my dorm room one evening, I began to be troubled and unable to concentrate. I couldn't dismiss it or ignore it. Something was wrong. I sensed that it had to do with my family, but didn't know what it could be. I called my parents, and they didn't indicate that anything was wrong, although they seemed a bit down. Nevertheless, I felt strongly compelled to pray for my whole family. I climbed the hill behind the dorm to a private spot and began praying for God to be with each member of my family. As I prayed, I felt a special need to pray for my sister-in-law. I had no idea why, but she was especially on my mind as I prayed. After I had finished praying, I felt relieved of my burden and was able return to my studies in peace.

Soon thereafter (my memory, imperfect as it is, tells me it was the very next day), I saw my sister-in-law in the office where she was employed on campus. I told her, "I don't know why, but yesterday I felt a strong compulsion to pray for the family, and especially for you. It was the strangest thing." She asked me at what time I had been led to pray. When I told her, tears welled up in her eyes. She said that at that very time, she was going through the trauma of a miscarriage.

It amazed me then, and it amazes me still. My sensitivity to God's Spirit had resulted in God compelling me to pray for something of which I could not humanly have any knowledge. I am convinced that God was using that moment to teach me the importance and power of prayer. God wanted me praying for that need, at that time, and it took a miracle for that to happen. Call it coincidence if you like, but I will never believe it to be so. Those who love God know His working when they see it.

I do not claim that this is the norm for all Christians at all times. The vast majority of the time we simply pray for the things well known to us, but God used this as a signpost for me, and I have never seen prayer the same way since. God made His point, and I readily admit that if I were always as close to God as I should be, perhaps I would have had more experiences like this than I have had.

Chapter 3

ANGEL HAND

For he will command his angels concerning you to guard you in all your ways...
(Psalm 91:11 NIV)

MY WIFE AND I were traveling from Idaho through Oregon to spend the holidays with our extended family. The drive could be treacherous through the mountain passes in the winter, but all the signs were that this trip wouldn't be bad. My '67 Mustang had notoriously bad drum brakes, but it seemed that the roads were mostly clear.

As we passed through one of the elevated stretches of the freeway, we came around a corner into a narrow gorge and suddenly realized that we were on black ice. We could see that ahead of us car after car had lost control and slid off the road and were stranded on the shoulder. A mother carrying a baby had stepped out of the car directly in front of us and was walking around the front of her car. I immediately began to carefully pump the brakes as I had been taught... No response! As a last ditch effort, I pushed the brake all the way down... Still nothing! As I anticipated the inevitable crash and potential tragedy, I told my wife, "We are going to hit!" I suddenly felt a jolt and the car came to a complete halt a foot short of the other car. There was no bare spot on the road or any other human explanation. I could just picture in my mind an angelic hand reaching down and stopping the car at that very moment.

Can I prove this supernatural explanation? Of course not. But there is little doubt in my mind that divine intervention was involved. I would never see the psalmist's explanation of God's protective hand through the guardianship of angels as just an abstract truth ever again. We were able to complete our trip without any further problems. Just thankful hearts and a strengthened faith.

Chapter 4

RAGGEDY MAN

Do not forget to entertain strangers, for by so doing some people have entertained angels without knowing it.
(Hebrews 13:2 NIV)

THE DAY BEGAN as many others as I pastored my small church in Boise, Idaho. I was sitting at my desk in the church office when a man came in to see me without an appointment. He looked like many others who came in asking for a handout from time to time. He was disheveled and dressed in ragged clothes. It would have been easy to hand him a card and send him on his way, but I welcomed him into my office, had him take a seat on the couch, and offered him a cup of coffee.

"What can I do for you today?" I asked him politely.

"I'm not sure," he replied.

Surprised by his answer, I asked, "What brought you here?"

"I was hitchhiking and felt like I was supposed to come here."

"And you don't know why?"

"No. Just that I needed to be here for some reason."

I perceived an opportunity for spiritual ministry. "Would you be interested to hear some good news from the Bible?" I asked. "The best gift I can give you is found there."

"Sure," he said nonchalantly.

So, I shared with him the truth about Jesus and how through faith in Him we can receive God's forgiveness and begin a new life. I asked him if he wanted to trust in Jesus and receive that gift. He quickly replied, "Yes, I do." I prayed with him and saw his demeanor change from that of a somewhat puzzled look when he came in to one of relaxation and contentment.

"Is that what you came for? Is that what you needed?" I asked him.

"Yes," he answered. "I didn't know what led me here, but that was it."

I asked him if there was anything else I could do for him, half expecting him to say he needed money as the skeptic in me was coming through.

"No, that's what I came for," he said, then began to quickly head out the door.

"Can't I offer you a ride somewhere?" I asked.

"No, I will just be on my way. Thank you very much."

I sat stunned for a while as he headed out of the building. Then I thought to myself that I should have insisted on giving him a ride or should have done something more for him. I quickly headed out the door to catch him before he was out of sight. He was nowhere to be found. It was as if he had disappeared into thin air.

As I contemplated what had just occurred, I found myself considering a couple of possibilities. Perhaps God had led this man to the church in a miraculous way. That was certainly a possibility. God will go to any length to reach a lost sheep. Jesus even talked about that. But how had the man disappeared so quickly? I began to consider another possibility. Could this have been a test? As the earlier mentioned verse in Hebrews says, angels have been known to appear in human form. Abraham himself experienced it. What if I had turned this man away and failed to be hospitable? What if I had been unwilling to share God's message with him? Whatever the case, I learned a lesson I would never forget. Hospitality reflects the heart of God. Our willingness to display it should never be based on outward appearances or personal comfort. God's gifts, whether physical or spiritual, are always meant to be shared. Hoarding them is an indication that we have never really learned the meaning of love and sacrifice, and you never know who you might be shortchanging.

Chapter 5

WELL DONE, SOLDIER

His master replied, "Well done, good and faithful servant!
You have been faithful with a few things;
I will put you in charge of many things.
Come and share your master's happiness!"
(Matthew 25:21 NIV)

I MENTIONED MY GRANDPA Phelps in the first chapter of this book. Needless to say, I was very close to him as a child prior to his passing. When visiting the farm, I stuck to him like glue because I wanted to be just like him. The back was his favorite piece of chicken, so it immediately became my favorite. (In case you were wondering, yes, this was the actual back of the chicken with the tail on it.) He liked milk toast on occasion for breakfast, so I had to try that, as well (I decided right away that I wasn't a fan). My mom told me that when I was a little squirt, I would sit in my high chair just yakking away and my grandpa would say, "That's my preacher boy!" Little did he know how prophetic that would be… Or did he? I will never forget him.

Many years later when Grandma Phelps passed away, Pastor Conradson officiated at the funeral. He had been my grandparents' pastor for many years and had even lived with them for a significant period of time (He never married). After the funeral, I rode back with him to the place where my family was staying.

It was a long drive, and we had a lot of time to talk. I learned much about my grandpa and grandma that I didn't know previously. The following is a story he told me about my grandpa that I have always cherished.

My grandpa served as a soldier in World War I, apparently after lying about his real age so that he could enlist for he was one year too young. He became a cook with the 491st Motor Truck Company. He was wounded and wound up in a military hospital as a result. While he was there, General Pershing, commander of the American Expeditionary Forces on the Western Front, paid a visit. He came to my grandpa's bed, leaned over, kissed him on the forehead, and said, "Well done, soldier." That deeply touched my grandpa. Here he was, a common foot soldier, being so honored by his supreme commanding officer. Pastor Conradson told me that this experience had always stuck with my grandpa for obvious reasons.

Some time later, after my grandpa had returned from the war, Pastor Conradson developed a severe illness that put him in the hospital. He told me that his illness was serious enough to be life threatening, and my grandpa came to pay him a visit and pray with him. After the visit ended, my grandpa headed out of the hospital room; however, he suddenly stopped at the door and seemed to be in deep thought for a moment. He then quickly turned around, returned to Pastor Conradson's bedside, kissed him on the forehead, and said, "Well done, soldier." Both of them knew what had moved my grandpa to perform this loving act.

Whenever I read the above verse in Matthew, this incident always comes to my mind. The parable Jesus told was meant to assure us that those who are faithful to Him will one day receive His personal commendation and reward. I have used my grandpa's story as the perfect sermon illustration when preaching from that passage. I am convinced that the circumstance of riding with Pastor Conradson after my grandma's funeral was no coincidence. In fact, Grandpa Phelps made such an impact on my life that I named my own son after him, and it is my sincere hope that in some small way I have learned to be like him.

Chapter 6

THE NUTCRACKER

...we must help the weak, remembering the words the Lord Jesus himself said: "It is more blessed to give than to receive."
(Acts 20:35 NIV)

IT WAS ONE of those years when Christmas fell on a Sunday. As a pastor, I always sought to balance church activities with a recognition of the importance of family time for the members of the congregation, especially around the holidays. I planned a short, informal church service on Christmas morning that would respect the need for families to get home early to pursue their family traditions. As I thought about my own family's personal time, I realized that this might be an opportunity for my wife and I to teach a valuable lesson to our children about giving and sacrifice.

There was an elderly lady named Helen in our congregation who lived by herself and had no family to spend the holidays with. She was pretty much a shut-in at that point in her life and had few friends. I am sure she had spent many Christmases alone. I had been told that she loved to collect decorative nutcrackers and display them at Christmastime. I thought of how nice it would be to stop by her little place and bring her a special gift of a new nutcracker after the Christmas service and spend a little time with her.

When I told my family that we were going to wait to open gifts and celebrate Christmas at our house until after this little mission of love, the children responded with the expected, "Aw, dad. Do we have to?" I was determined to ignore their pleas and we headed to Helen's place across town. She lived in a modest little one bedroom apartment that could barely accommodate our family of five, but she was very happy to welcome us in.

When Helen opened our gift, her eyes lit up. You would think from her reaction that we had brought her the greatest gift she had ever received. She gave us a heartfelt thanks and was delighted to add the nutcracker to her collection. We spent some nice time chatting together and I closed our time by saying a prayer for her. My wife tells me there were tears in her eyes as we wished her a Merry Christmas and went on our way.

Truth be told, what was intended as an opportunity to minister to a member of our congregation and to give an object lesson about priorities to our children became a powerful learning experience for me, as well. You see, I almost missed this opportunity because I cherish my family time at Christmas and knew the children would not be pleased at the disruption to our normal schedule, especially when the church service was already something they had to patiently endure before opening gifts at home. I had come very close to deciding against it. I am so thankful I followed through, knowing it was the right thing to do. I will never forget the delight in Helen's face that day and the joy it gave me for us to be there with her. My selfish desires seemed so trivial in comparison. I learned firsthand in a new and important way that it is truly more blessed to give than to receive. Especially at Christmastime.

Chapter 7

THE COFFEE SHOP

...Paul...was reasoning in the synagogue with the Jews and the God-fearing Gentiles, and in the market place every day with those who happened to be present.
(Acts 17:16-17 NASB)

FAIRLY EARLY IN my ministry as a pastor, I came to the realization that I wasn't following Paul's pattern of ministry. I was sharing God's truth with God's people in the church, but not very much in the community of people outside of the church. I was becoming more and more isolated from the "real world." It is easy for this to happen when you spend most of your time studying in the church office and shepherding the people in your congregation. After all, the sheep must be fed and cared for. But spiritual leaders in the church are also called upon to be examples to the flock in sharing their faith with those who do not know God.

I began to get more active in the community, serving as our neighborhood association president, participating in our kids' schools, leading a fitness group, and more. I will never forget when I was interviewed for the neighborhood association presidency and was asked by someone, "What do you do?"

"I am a pastor," I said.

One of the other residents said, "I don't think you are. I think you are a really nice guy."

It took me a minute or two to realize that she thought I had said I was something that sounds like pastor, but starts with a "b" and ends with a "d." I got a pretty good laugh over that! But the thing that really opened me up to developing relationships outside of the church was when I began taking my study materials to a coffee shop named Coffee Critic in the afternoons and connecting with people there. Little did I know how God would use my experiences to give me a whole new perspective on ministry.

Now you must understand that this new avenue for sharing with people in the community began at a time when coffee shops were just beginning to be popular in the Boise area. They offered a unique place for people to socialize and discuss issues. It wasn't long before I got to know the owner of Coffee Critic pretty well. She knew that I was a pastor and enjoyed discussing spiritual issues with people. She also knew that I had a favorite table in the corner with a nice view of the adjacent lake. Over time, she saved the table for me when she knew I would be coming in and would even direct people to me who were showing interest in religion and spirituality. She would tell them, "There's the guy you need to talk to about those things." I don't believe she was a Christian or necessarily religious herself, so this made for an interesting scenario. The place was frequented by all kinds of people, including Goths, New Agers, and Wiccans. There were good opportunities to discuss spiritual issues and beliefs with some of these people and I learned right away that many of those one would think would be the most closed-minded and even hostile to Christian beliefs were actually friendly and easy to talk to. In other words, I learned that a lot of our stereotypes are actually way off base. My second office (as I came to call it) became an open door for developing relationships and sharing my faith.

When the coffee shop was sold and eventually became a restaurant, I moved to another coffee shop nearby and continued my pattern of ministry there. As the leadership of my church was re-examining our approach to ministry to make our services more "seeker friendly," I took the opportunity to interview people I got to know (with their consent, of course) who were not church attenders and to ask them what things turned them off about churches and what changes would appeal to them. I expected a lot of responses to focus on the Christian belief system and what they didn't like about it, things which we would never change. Instead, I found that most of them didn't like having to dress up, didn't like the judgmental spirit and lack of friendliness in churches they had visited, couldn't relate to the out-of-date church music, and didn't like the impersonal way that the Bible was taught without opportunity for discussion among other things. All valid criticisms.

This turned out to be invaluable input for us to reshape our church ministry in meaningful ways. For example, we went to a casual "come as you are" emphasis for dress, put the sermon outline and verses on the screen and on an insert in the bulletin to assist with those who might struggle to find things in the Bible, updated our music with a contemporary worship band, and included a sharing segment as part of our worship. The Bible clearly teaches that if Christ and His cross are a stumbling block to people, so be it. We should never compromise our convictions, but all of our manmade obstacles should be removed. God used my coffee shop experience to not only add a dimension to my personal ministry, but to revolutionize our entire church's outreach to our community.

The story doesn't end there. One of the "regulars" that I got to know at this new coffee shop would often ask me questions like, "Why do you believe there is so much suffering in the world? Why would a loving God allow people to suffer? Why are there so many different religions? Don't they all say essentially the same things?" I would answer as best I could. I remember telling her I wasn't a prophet or anything, to which she replied, "You are the closest thing to a prophet I know." She showed a keen interest in spiritual things and even transcribed my commentary on the Gospel of John onto a computer disk for me. She became a regular attender at our church and eventually professed faith in Jesus. Believe it or not, she later bought the coffee shop, and my wife became her business partner for a period of time to help her run it. Students from Boise Bible College would even provide Christian music on Saturday evenings for the customers. Unfortunately, this didn't last, and the coffee shop eventually had to close down, but we will never forget our experiences there.

I must add a little postscript to all of this. I still frequent a coffee shop in town. That's where I am at this very moment as I write these words. A couple of months ago, I was sitting here at one of the long tables next to a couple of college students. When I got up to leave, one of them asked me if I got a lot of work done. I explained that I was writing a book and she asked what it was about. When I explained it to her, she said, "So, it is kind of like your faith journey, isn't it?" I said that it was. She responded by telling me, "You won't believe this, but I was just now thinking about the fact that I ought to keep a journal of my own faith journey!" I encouraged her to do so, of course. God was using my book to inspire someone else before it was even published! And all of these things only happened because God opened my eyes to a new marketplace for sharing with people. Not to mention it doesn't hurt that I love coffee.

Chapter 8

MAKING THE NEWS

Do not be overcome by evil, but overcome evil with good.
(Romans 12:21 NIV)

OUR CHURCH DAYCARE had had an unfortunate accident. One of the children had broken a window in one of the classrooms. Fortunately, no one was hurt. The broken glass was quickly cleaned up and the repairman from the glass company called out. We always replaced broken windows with safety glass, so the repairman told us it would have to be special ordered and would take a couple of days to finish the job. We boarded up the window and things seemed fine. Little did we know then what the consequences would be.

The next morning, we found that someone had broken into the church through the window that was boarded up and had vandalized the entire facility. Paint was splashed throughout the building, including on the large collection of books in my personal office. Sound equipment in the worship center was knocked over and damaged. The fire extinguishers throughout the building were emptied of their contents everywhere. Satanic messages and symbols were painted on the wall, leading us to believe that a Satanic cult of some kind may have been involved. The police were notified, of course, and took a complete report. Such an occurrence was very unusual in Boise, Idaho, so it became a big news story on the local news. To add insult to injury, the church was broken into again the very next night and all of the food in the kitchen was dumped and spread all over the floor and thrown on the cabinets. It had not been noticed the day before that an extra set of van keys had been taken, but after the kitchen was ransacked, the daycare van was taken for a joy ride. The fabric throughout was torn up and the van was found by the police department abandoned somewhere in town. The police were obviously very concerned that we were likely the target of a hate crime and began patrolling the area frequently at night.

 The church congregation worked hard to clean up as much of the mess as possible the next day. The insurance company sent out a claim representative soon thereafter to survey the damage and begin the process of repair and replacement of the damaged items. I did some news interviews and prayed for wisdom in my response to the situation in order for our church to present a positive witness to the community. I thought the worst was over, but it was not to be so.

 A few weeks later, I got a call from our daycare director letting me know that someone had called her after she left the building (she was the last one out) and that it was on fire! The fire department had been notified and when I arrived, the fire trucks were on site and putting out the fire. It had already destroyed the entry area of the building, but by the grace of God and the hard work of the firemen, the worship center, offices, and classrooms had been preserved with only smoke damage. It was ultimately determined that it was an act of arson.

 Needless to say, now we were not only a local news story, but a regional and even a national one. It seemed clear that someone was out to destroy us. I was interviewed so many times that my face was becoming familiar to many more people in the community. I could tell that some people I didn't know thought they knew me, but weren't sure why. While all this additional damage was being repaired (including some asbestos removal when the remainder of the entry ceiling was pulled down), we had to meet outdoors in the adjacent park. The news media did a report on our outdoor Sunday service and interviewed a number of our church members. I was so proud of their reaction to the crisis. No one expressed any hostility or desire for vengeance. They made it clear that the church is the people, not the building, and that we were praying for the perpetrators. I was so glad my sermons on these subjects had not gone unheard, although I am sure many of those in the congregation had come to the proper understanding on their own.

All of this had brought a heartwarming reaction from the community. Words of encouragement came from people all over Boise. Many offered help and others sent money gifts to help with the repair costs. The most touching display of concern came from the pastor of a Black church in town. I had never met him, but he showed up at the church, shed tears for us, and prayed a touching prayer for God's grace to be shown to us. His church had taken an offering for us and he gave us the generous gift.

After a couple of weeks, we were able to regain use of our worship center and renew services there. Our first service back in the facility was accompanied by a news crew. I spoke from the Book of Matthew where Jesus taught His disciples to love their enemies and pray for those who persecute them. We included a time of prayer for those who had perpetrated the crimes against us. The news report we watched later was very positive and we were glad to have the opportunity to display to the community what we believe Christian love is all about.

In a relatively short amount of time, the police received information that led to the arrest of several teenagers for the vandalism of the church facility and van. They had decided it would be fun to trash a church and make it look like it was done by Satanists. They all pleaded guilty and at sentencing the judge required that they all publicly apologize to the congregation during a Sunday service and do a number of hours of community service, preferably at the church if we so desired. It was obvious they were very nervous when they came to apologize to the church, probably expecting to be met with some level of hatred and rebuke; however, when they apologized, I told them before the congregation that we forgave them and loved them. The congregation received them with open arms, invited them to attend church, and to be a part of our youth group. We had them work to fulfill their community service requirement by working alongside us as we redid the landscaping around the church, and we had great opportunities to share with them.

It turned out the arson was committed by an eight year old boy named Anthony who thought it would be fun to light a bush by the front entrance, not realizing that it would catch the building on fire. There was no connection to the vandalism at all. His parents were spending time in jail, and he was staying with his grandfather who ran a fruit stand. While his grandfather was working, Anthony was left at home and free to roam unsupervised. He was also required by the authorities to do some community service and to receive weekly counseling from me at the church. We put him to work doing various tasks for the daycare under my supervision and he actually seemed to enjoy our times together. In fact, my family was able to take him with us to our church family camp and we treated him just like he was one of our own children. He even began calling us "mom and dad" while at camp. Soon thereafter, his mom got out of jail and the last we heard she had come to faith in Christ and was taking Anthony with her to attend a good church across town. We were gratified to hear this.

When the repair work was completed on our facility, we scheduled a special celebration service and invited all those who had helped us and contributed gifts for our recovery. We asked St. Paul Baptist Church (the Black church mentioned earlier) to form a combined choir with our singers and choose the music for the service. It worked out beautifully. For one thing, we learned how to sing with a little more soul! The turnout was good, and it was a very special time for all of us. When it was all said and done, what began as an extremely trying situation ended up being a wonderful blessing. We had the privilege of showing and receiving genuine Christian love in the midst of persecution. And I saw more clearly than ever what it really means for good to triumph over evil.

CHAPTER 9
A STRANGE ENCOUNTER

Let your conversation be always full of grace, seasoned with salt, so that you may know how to answer everyone.
(Colossians 4:6 NIV)

IT WAS A nice summer day when a group of six young adults (four males and two females) entered the church facility and came to my office asking to talk with me. They all wore the same black, loose fitting clothes and had the same short haircuts. Clearly an intentional unisex look. I suspected right away that they were part of a strange religious group or cult. They seemed very kind and polite, and I was happy to speak with them, so I invited them to join me in the church library, which also served as a meeting room for small groups. They shared with me that they had found spiritual truth that coincided with the Bible and Christianity and wanted to share it with me. I told them I was always willing to discuss spiritual things with people from all kinds of backgrounds and experiences. So began what I can only describe as a strange, unexpected encounter.

Different members of the group shared with me that they were some of the twelve disciples of Jesus reborn into this life. As I recall, three claimed to be the disciples Peter, James and John who comprised Jesus's inner circle. They told me they were followers of two leaders who were prophets and one of which had come to be the new Christ who would complete Jesus's unfinished work. They also seemed to believe that they were in the end time spoken of in the Book of Revelation in the Bible. My heart went out to them because I could see that they were sincere in their pursuit of spiritual truth, but had been greatly misled by a cult leader with a Messiah complex. I shared with them that I, too, had an interest in the end times spoken of in the Bible and that Jesus had warned that at that time "false Christs and false prophets will appear" as recorded in the Book of Matthew. I shared with them that they had been misled by a false Messiah and that the only true Messiah was the Jesus of the Bible and their faith needed to be in Him alone. I warned them that the direction in which they were headed, while well-intentioned, was a path that would actually lead them away from God. After they saw that I was clearly unconvinced by their claims, they quietly slipped out and went their way.

I thought little more about this encounter until a news report caught my attention sometime later. A group of cultists in California had committed suicide coinciding with the passing by of Halley's Comet. They were followers of a Messianic figure named Marshall Applewhite and believed that they were passing from this physical existence to be picked up by an alien UFO and taken off to a higher plain of existence. As I watched the various news reports, it suddenly struck me. Could my strange visitors have been a part of this group? The more I learned about the Heaven's Gate cult, the more the teachings were much the same. Then came the clincher: I was sure I could recognize some of the individuals I met with as pictures and videos of the group's activities were shown. But why were they in Boise, Idaho, and why did they pay me a visit? As I have researched the group further, I have found that they had connected with churches and received donations from some of them at one time and had also done some proselytizing in the Northwest after a period of seclusion. Other than that, I have no explanation.

The thing that struck me after this realization was the fact that God may have used this encounter as an opportunity (perhaps a final one) for these individuals to be warned about the direction they were headed and to be presented with the truth. My willingness to reach out to them in love in spite of their strange beliefs and almost robotic behavior left me with a clear conscience and a realization that we must take the opportunities we are given, no matter how unconventional, to share God's truth with others. My hope is that perhaps one of the group that met with me may have listened to my words and left the cult before it's terrible end, but I cannot be sure of that. The important lesson I learned was that you never know what the future may hold and the opportunity that you might have to shape it. Another signpost along the way.

Chapter 10

THE OUTCASTS

Let the outcasts of Moab stay with you;
Be a hiding place to them from the destroyer...
(Isaiah 16:4 NASB)

MY CHURCH HAD begun to be actively involved in ministering to refugees and I had personally committed some of my ministry time to local refugee services as part of my ministry. We assisted refugees from Albania, Afghanistan, Iraq, and Ethiopia. Later, my wife and I personally sponsored an Ethiopian family who lived with us until they were able to be on their own. They were technically legal immigrants because they had lived and worked in Belgium for a period of time before coming to the States and could not be sponsored by an organization. They are now US Citizens and continue to be a special part of our family. All of these people had escaped persecution in their own countries and fled to seek a new life in the US, but they awoke in me a new appreciation of God's blessings on our country and a compassion for those less fortunate.

Kirov was an Albanian refugee who was the first we assisted as a church. I will never forget his love of our country and all it represents. At that time, Albania was the poorest country in Europe and when communism fell, he was able to return and delighted in bringing back to his former homeland every item he could purchase to show off his newfound wealth. This became a bit of a problem when he attempted to walk onto the plane with a large color TV on a cart and had to be convinced that he would have to pay extra and have it added as regular luggage. Kirov was often a handful, but my fondest memory was when I mentioned Independence Day in the Sunday church service and he immediately came to the front of the church and insisted that we all sing the "Battle Hymn of the Republic" together as he led out.

Muhsen and Maysoon were refugees from Iraq. They were devout Muslims (Muhsen was even considered to be one of the "sons of the prophet"—a descendant of Mohammed himself), but had to leave their country because they were suffering persecution at the hands of the more radical elements of Islam and from the government itself. Saddam Hussein had taken their son at a young age to be trained as part of his youth brigade (sort of the equivalent of the Hitler Youth in Germany). They had to flee to this country without him. I remember when I first met them they made a point of communicating to me by gestures and pictures (their English was still limited) that they wanted to be at peace with Christians. They came to consider my personal family to be their American family and we often shared meals together in the traditional Iraqi way, seated on the floor with spicy food spread out on a blanket. I even had the privilege of being invited to one of their Muslim gatherings on a Saturday night to answer questions about the meaning of Christianity.

The amazing thing was that we began to see a number of Muslims attending our church services each Sunday. They communicated to me that we were willing to do more for them than the Muslim mosque would ever do. Maysoon asked me for a Bible in Arabic so she could translate my sermon notes. A Muslim from Afghanistan brought a friend fluent in English to my discipleship class to translate my teaching into Farsi. But the most amazing thing happened the Sunday after the terrorist attack on 9/11. We typically had a time of open sharing during the worship time in our Sunday service and Muhsen stood up and spoke in halting English, saying, "I very sorry for what Muslims did... It is wrong and I want to say I against it."

Muhsen and Maysoon later moved away, and we have only been able to keep in touch on a limited basis; however, we were gratified to hear that they were able to retrieve their son after the US forces overthrew the government in Iraq and Muhsen eventually became an interpreter for the US Military while Maysoon trained to be a nurse. I have learned from all of the refugees we have been able to help that I should never take for granted the freedom and prosperity we enjoy in this country. But more than that, God taught me that as one who was once a spiritual outcast (as are we all), He has enfolded me in His arms of love and expects me to do the same for all those who are outcasts in this world.

Chapter 11

THE MISSION TRIP

He upholds the cause of the oppressed and gives food to the hungry. The LORD sets prisoners free... (Psalm 146:7 NIV)

WHEN I WAS asked to help lead a mission trip to the LA area in California for the Christian college I had attended, I was happy to say yes. My youngest daughter attended the college and was on the team. It would be a great opportunity to minister together. A new adventure. Little did I know what I was really getting into.

We were going to be based in the Hawthorne area, assisting a church there in their outreach effort in the ghetto. It was already dark when we arrived at the church after a long van trip, and the first thing I noticed was that the church was located in what can only be properly described as a walled compound. Police helicopters were flying overhead, their spotlights focusing on some kind of activity on the ground not far away. It felt like I was entering a third world country. The coming days would only reinforce that impression.

The pastor of the church briefed us on what we would be doing each day while we were there. He also told us there had been a street shooting nearby and we should be careful when being out and about. He discouraged us from wearing certain colors of clothing because of their gang association. He informed us that the events of the week would lead up to a concert being offered free to the public by a well-known singing artist who was a Christian.

After being briefed, we were led to the place where we would be spending the night. It was a large classroom with mats on the floor to sleep on. Pretty rustic to say the least. When we began our ministry the next day, my eyes were opened to the life in the ghetto. It was so foreign to my experiences in the conservative, low-crime city of Boise, Idaho. When we passed out the invitations to the coming concert in the neighborhoods surrounding the church, we were asked to knock on doors and make a personal connection whenever possible. What I discovered right away was that the houses typically had barred windows and doors and that people were wary about someone coming to their door. One house had a peephole through which the resident advised us to please put the invitation through a small slot in the wall. I thought this was crazy. These poor people lived in constant fear of strangers and felt a need to be careful when coming out of their homes. Not since doing volunteer work in juvenile correctional institutions while in college had I had this kind of feeling.

Part of our ministry involved distributing food to various needy areas around the city. We brought in a couple of trucks and set up tables right in the middle of Skid Row. As the food was set out, street people from all over immediately worked their way to where we were and picked up their meal. They were usually very thankful for our willingness to help them and readily accepted the literature we handed out with the meal. As the team shared a Christian witness with various people in the area, the reactions were unpredictable. My daughter told me a transgender prostitute had asked her if I was available. She told her I was a pastor and was already taken. We got a good laugh over that later on.

On another occasion, we made sandwiches and distributed them, along with some literature, to the vagrants at MacArthur Park. The only thing I knew about the park was the Richard Harris song by the same name (a friend told me later that he grew up in the area and used to play there when he was a kid). Whatever positive image I may have had in my mind was dashed upon arriving there. It had become a notorious hangout for drug addicts, and we were warned ahead of time not to wear any open-toed shoes because of the hypodermic needles that might be lying around. Without going into any sickening detail, the restrooms there were the most disgusting of any I had ever seen. But these people were precious souls who needed hope in their lives, so we were happy to share the love of God with them.

Perhaps the most eye-opening experience I had on the trip was the volunteer work we did at a youth center in the middle of the Compton area. When we arrived, we drove into a walled compound that contained recreational facilities including a full-length outdoor basketball court. We were given a detailed orientation by the director of the facility. He told us, "See this center spot? To the right is the territory of one gang and to the left the territory of another. This youth center is considered by both gangs to be neutral territory. Do not go outside these walls. The risk is too great." This was sobering, of course, but we were able to have a good time getting to know some of the participants there and sharing with them as we had opportunity. I was past my prime (to say the least) when playing basketball with the teens there, but I have to admit I was pleased when I was told by some of them, "It's cool that a pastor your age can play some pretty good ball!"

The last experience I want to share was the report I received from my daughter about one of the outreach efforts she participated in. Some of the female college students on our team volunteered to go to the "red-light district" to share and pass out literature there. The sex trafficking of underage girls is common there and the team was equipped with pamphlets explaining where they could get help. As my daughter was talking with a girl she guessed was about fifteen or sixteen years of age, she noticed that her pimp showed up and had his eye on them. A dangerous situation to say the least. She asked the girl if she wanted the pamphlet she had in her hand. The girl simply pointed to the ground, meaning, "I can't be seen taking the literature, but I will pick it up later on." So, my daughter dropped it and left.

God opened my eyes to the fact that not everyone enjoys the "normal life" I enjoy. In fact, most of the people in the world are probably living more like those we ministered to. For the first time, I could understand what it was like for missionaries working in third world countries and the sacrifices they are making. My heart was moved to realize in a greater way the struggles many have with addiction and mental illness, and how many others live in a constant state of fear and have feelings of hopelessness. On a positive note, I also saw many transformed lives through God's work among the people there. Many of those we worked with had, themselves, once lived similar lives and come to faith in Christ. They were a constant inspiration to me. The bottom line: I left California with a greater sense of mission to a world in need. A much needed signpost along the way.

Chapter 12

THE CUP OF COFFEE

Look at the birds of the air, they do not sow or reap or store away in barns, and yet your heavenly Father feeds them. Are you not much more valuable than they?
(Matthew 6:26 NIV)

WE WERE DEAD broke. Because of the financial struggles of the church I pastored, I had taken a significant pay cut. Like many people, we were living month to month without any money left over. Sometimes the money ran out before the end of the month. I hardly claim that all of the financial decisions I had made were wise, but I was trying to be a good steward. I found myself on the way to the office and my custom was to pick up a cup of coffee at a drive-through coffee place on the way, but there was no money in the account and only a little change in my pocket. It sounds a little silly, but my prayer was, "God, I just need a cup of coffee this morning. Please help me get one." I had some additional change (mostly pennies) in the ash tray in the car, so I pulled it out and added it to the change in my pocket. I couldn't remember the exact amount required for a 12 ounce coffee, but I pulled up to the coffee place and hoped for the best. When I was told the amount I owed, it was exactly (to the penny) the amount I had scraped together!

I don't mean to say that this was the result of a great act of faith on my part, but it was clear to me that God wanted to teach me an important lesson. He knows my every need and cares deeply even about the little things. As the above Scripture says, if He cares about the birds, how much more He cares about me! Even about a cup of coffee I wanted but didn't really need! You see, what I was really needing at that point in my life was some encouragement. Some sense that God hadn't forgotten about me. That He understood my situation and really was in control of everything. I have never forgotten that moment, so it clearly accomplished its purpose.

Chapter 13

IT'S A WONDERFUL LIFE

*Let us not become weary in doing good, for at the
proper time we will reap a harvest if we do not give up.
(Galatians 6:9 NIV)*

I HAD COME TO a dark point in my life. My father had passed away. The church I pastored was struggling. The daycare ministry we had operated for many years as an outreach to the community had to close down for financial reasons. Many people were discouraged, and we were losing members, including a number of them in key positions in the church. I began to feel like a failure in leadership. Depression was setting in. It was the Christmas season, so my oldest daughter, in an effort to cheer me up, offered to take her mom and me to a special showing of the classic Christmas movie *It's a Wonderful Life* at the Egyptian Theater downtown. I had never actually watched the full movie, so I was glad for the opportunity to see it for the first time.

As the plot of the movie unfolded, I could immediately relate to the main character, George Bailey (played by James Stewart). He questioned whether or not he had made a difference in this life and whether or not it was worth it to go on living. In similar fashion, I had found myself crying and praying for God to take me out of this life because I had felt so worthless. As you probably know, the movie has a happy ending as an angel shows George that his life was, indeed, worthwhile, and the people of his community make it known to him that he is loved and appreciated.

On the way home from the movie, I commented that I wished that life was really like that, that people really appreciated what I or anyone else had done for them. My experience had been that people took me for granted and rarely expressed such appreciation. I was in a bad place, obviously, and feeling sorry for myself. Unbeknownst to me, my daughter took this on as a challenge to prove me wrong. With help from her younger sister, she began a project that would change my whole outlook on life.

The project my daughter embarked on involved contacting many of the people whose lives I had impacted down through the years and having them write down an expression of what I had meant to them and send it to her. She then put these into a big album that was a kind of "This Is Your Life" reminder. Here are a few of the quotes found in the album:

"You've been a father to me. If it weren't for you and your wonderful family, I don't think I'd be alive today."

"I just wanted you to know that if not for you coming to our door, I don't know where I would be now."

"You encouraged me so much. You were always saying, "Hi," smiling, and made the time to meet with me and gave me good counsel and prayers."

"Thank you for loving and pouring into the people closest to me, who shaped me and made me who I am. You were probably the closest thing to a second dad to me. You always treated your

girls with gentleness and love, and I completely respect your quiet leadership by example."

"Without you, we wouldn't have had the most level-headed, full-of-integrity, Spirit-led, and patient guy around to lead us through the tough stuff we've had down through the years."

"You gave me a job, you invited me to your church, and you even opened up your home to my family and I. You have given so much to so many people and loved us unconditionally, never once did you expect or ask for anything in return."

"I can't tell you how many times you calmed my nerves when I was ready to quit."

"Thank you doesn't sound like enough for all the love, hugs, and support you've given me through my life."

"I loved when you would teach through the Old Testament and other passages. I long for God's Word because of those years."

"When my world was shattered last summer, I was very lost and didn't know where to start to make sense of things; however, I did know that you were a person I needed to go to. For knowledge, strength, and courage."

"You have been such an important friend and mentor to my husband. I don't think that his first steps into vocational ministry would have been the same without you."

"Your gentle demeanor and honest strength of character that you get from your faith radiates to all who meet you."

"You taught me how to love, to laugh, what it was to have a healthy father figure in my life, and most importantly taught me about our Heavenly Father and Jesus."

"Please never forget the works that God has done through you. You are one of the kindest, most Christ-like men that I know, and I hope you never lose that fire."

Please don't take this as bragging on myself. In all honesty, I could also fill an album full of all my weaknesses and failures, and I never forget that God ultimately gets the credit for all the good stuff, and I am solely responsible for the bad. But God used this experience to remind me that my life and ministry had made a difference. Whenever I feel a little down, I just pull out the album and shed some tears. But these are tears of joy.

Chapter 14

HOUSE MIRACLE

And my God will meet all your needs according to his glorious riches in Christ Jesus.
(Philippians 4:19 NIV)

BECAUSE OF OUR continuing financial struggles due to a significant loss of income, my wife and I were seeking to restructure our home mortgage to avoid losing our home. I could no longer make the house payment without some assistance. Humanly speaking, the odds seemed small, but we were working with the mortgage company to see if we could get the payment lowered. I also was working what amounted to three part-time jobs at the time and could no longer afford the exploding cost of self-financed medical insurance. One of my jobs was as a security officer at a senior living campus. As far as I had been able to ascertain, the security positions had always been filled on a part-time basis. To get benefits, I would have to work full-time (at least thirty-two hours a week). I told my manager that I would need to be able to go full-time or I would be forced to find another job with benefits. She kindly said she would talk to the director, but that he might need to get corporate approval. This all sets the stage for one of the most miraculous things I have ever experienced in my life.

My wife and I had been praying for God to meet our needs as promised in verses like the one above. We didn't know how, but we were looking to God to provide for us. When I received a letter from the mortgage company (name withheld as a courtesy), I hoped it would be something positive about our effort to restructure the mortgage. What it actually said blew me away. These are the exact words in the letter:

We are pleased to let you know that we have approved your Home Equity account for a principal forgiveness program offered by _____ as part of its recent settlement with the Department of Justice. You will receive a full forgiveness of the remaining principal balance of $63,959.28 on your Home Equity account. This means that you will no longer owe this amount, and we will also waive any outstanding fees and accrued interest.

I have to admit that my first thought was that this must be a scam or something. I contacted the mortgage company and they verified that it was legitimate. I was awestruck at the power of God. I had never heard of such a thing happening. The human reason behind it was that the former mortgage holder, bought out by the current one, had pulled some illegal shenanigans and was being penalized by the federal government, but I knew full well that God was behind the whole thing. I was chosen out of thousands of mortgage holders to receive this settlement money and as a result would be able to stay in my home. To my knowledge, I had not been personally harmed by the actions of the previous mortgage company. This was clearly a providential act by a Sovereign God. I was also informed by the mortgage company that there could be tax implications if Congress did not renew a special provision at the end of the year. It was renewed for another year! As if this wasn't enough, I was informed the very next day that I had been approved to go to full-time status at my security job and would be eligible for benefits. This signpost in my life clearly read, "I meant it when I said I would meet all your needs out of my great wealth"—God.

Chapter 15

THE HUMBLING

Humble yourselves, therefore, under God's mighty hand, that he may lift you up in due time.
(1 Peter 5:6 NIV)

I WAS NO LONGER the pastor of a church due to negative circumstances that will be described in the next chapter. As discussed in the last chapter, I had been hired to do security at a senior living community. Part of the job involved doing security rounds throughout the campus, both inside and outside of the buildings. Since this included independent living, assisted living, and nursing care facilities, it involved a lot of miles of walking. One evening as I was doing the walkthrough in the independent living area, I noticed that one of the residents had spilled a large amount of liquid detergent on the floor of one of the laundry rooms. The cleanup would normally be the responsibility of the maintenance crew, but since I worked the swing shift no one was available. I knew that if I left the mess to be cleaned up the next day there would be a risk of a resident slipping and falling before someone could get to it. That could be a particularly dangerous situation with seniors, so I knew I had to clean it up myself.

If you have ever attempted to clean up liquid detergent off of a floor, you know how difficult that can be. It is a slimy mess that must be wiped up and then the residue cleaned off with water. And this was no small spill. It seemed like half a bottle of detergent. As I was cleaning up the mess on my arthritic knees (the result of many years of being an avid runner and two surgical knee repairs), I couldn't help but think of the biblical declaration, "How the mighty have fallen!" I had been a pastor shepherding a flock of people, loved and respected. Speaking God's message each Sunday. Bringing healing to wounded souls. Now I had lost all of that and was doing a janitor's work instead. But then another thought came to my mind: This is exactly where God wants me to be! On my hurting knees, scrubbing the floor with no one to see my efforts. You see, God was destroying my pride and teaching me the importance of humility. Just what I needed, and I made sure to thank Him for it.

Chapter 16

DESIRES FULFILLED

*Delight yourself in the LORD
and he will give you the desires of your heart.
(Psalm 37:4 NIV)*

BECAUSE OF THE struggles we were going through as a church, I sought a new church with the same essential beliefs as ours that was in need of a facility to meet in (our building was paid for) and would be interested in a merger. I felt this could breathe some new life into our congregation and be a big help to a new church start. I found one that fit the bill, so long as I was willing to take a secondary role in the pulpit. It was a sacrifice I was willing to make. The merge itself went smoothly. It was a beautiful thing for two congregations to come together as one. We were able to remake the entire worship center in only one week's time before meeting together for the first service together. There was a sense of excitement over the future and what God was going to do.

Unfortunately, I found in due time that the co-pastor arrangement was not working out and I was gradually being squeezed out of my place of influence. The younger pastor seemed threatened by my presence and showed some strong narcissistic tendencies that made me very uncomfortable. I found myself to be more and more unhappy with the arrangement and less and less able to minister effectively. I was eventually removed from the payroll to make room for the other pastor to go full-time and asked to continue on an unpaid basis. After a discussion with my family and some outside counsel, I decided that due to the circumstances and to avoid creating conflict in the church, I would notify the leadership that I would be leaving the church and slipped quickly and quietly away. I had always pictured a big retirement party and congregational thanks for many years of service. But it was not to be.

As you can imagine, this was one of the most difficult times in my life and ministry. I was deeply hurt by the way things ended at the church after so many years of ministry. My wife and I spent a year healing, regrouping, and seeking God's will for the next step in our lives. We felt aimless and fought feelings of bitterness. We visited some churches during this time, but didn't find a good fit. We eventually started a home group (it really was a small house church) with some others who were either disconnected from a church or were old friends looking for some additional fellowship.

After some time, we were invited by friends to visit a church that was another new church start. We felt connected right away. The younger pastor immediately sought my input, counsel, and assistance. I became a valued part of his sermon prep group and was asked to fill the pulpit from time to time. It was exactly the kind of thing I was looking for as a final phase of my ministry. The beauty of it all is the fact that God fulfilled the desire of my heart in a way I could never have imagined. We committed to the church and included our home group as part of the church's small group ministry.

Early on in the new church, I had the opportunity to tell my story to the pastor, so he was aware of my disappointment in how things ended at my previous church. My first time speaking to the new and growing congregation was my first time speaking in a church service in a couple of years. It was especially meaningful to me because all three of my children were able to be there, including my son who was in the Navy. After I gave the message, the pastor stood before the church and said, "I hadn't really planned this, but I feel led to say something. The man who spoke to you this morning pastored a church for over thirty-five years and had to leave under difficult circumstances. He was never properly thanked for his many years of ministry. I think we should give him a heartfelt expression of thanks right now." The congregation gave me a rousing and lengthy ovation that brought tears to the eyes of my entire family.

You see, it really is true that if we delight in God, He will not only give us the proper desires, but also bring them to fruition. Even if it is in a manner different from what we had planned. We have been told His ways are not our ways, that is true, but His ways are always the best ways. Thankfully, I see that more clearly now than ever.

PART TWO: YOUR JOURNEY

CHAPTER 17

ARE YOU ON THE JOURNEY?

PERHAPS IF YOU have read this far you have found yourself wondering what all of this means to you. If you have no meaningful relationship with God, the answer is that it may mean little to you and you may choose to read no further. If you aren't on the journey, then you have no need for signposts. I will only say to you, I believe you are missing out on those things that truly make life meaningful. Leave God out of the picture and nothing really makes much sense. Put God and His Word into the picture and everything fits together and there are answers to life's deepest questions. But the choice is yours.

If you are on this spiritual journey with me, then I believe that you, too, can have key moments in your life that serve as signposts for you. For the Christian, following Christ means a lifelong commitment to this journey until we move on to the greater realities to be found in the life beyond this life. My goal for you is for you to keep your spiritual eyes open and view life as a wonderful adventure with many lessons to be learned along the way. It is, at times, very difficult, even painful, but it is never drudgery for the one who sees God at work.

I have come to be convinced that for many Christians their faith is just a set of beliefs to be argued over, but not a personal daily interaction with God. Let's face it, we can all pretty easily find ourselves going through the motions when it comes to spiritual living, but without our hearts really being in it. That's why God must wake us up at times by bringing the spiritual realities to our attention through life's experiences. In fact, we are told in the Scriptures that some of the trials we go through are for the very purpose of God giving us a wake-up call when we are ignoring Him. It hurts, but it is for our good. As you may have noticed from my own experiences, very often the most important lessons we learn are learned during the toughest times in our lives. God refuses to be ignored. He loves us that much.

    If this all makes sense to you, read on…

CHAPTER 18

THE IMPORTANCE OF WATERSHED MOMENTS

...In the future, when your children ask you, "What do these stones mean? Tell them that the flow of the Jordan was cut off before the ark of the covenant of the LORD... These stones are to be a memorial to the people of Israel forever."
(Joshua 4:6-7 NIV)

THE NATION OF Israel faced a seemingly insurmountable obstacle. The Jordan River was at flood stage. It stood between them and the land God had promised them. Everything depended on them getting across, and at their time of need, God performed an amazing miracle on their behalf: He stopped the flow of the river upstream until all of the people were able to cross on dry ground. Nature's God overruled the normal laws of nature. The Israelites must have been astounded and thankful, but God knew human nature and our tendency to forget over time, so He gave them some unusual instructions. He told twelve men, one from each tribe, to go back and each pick up a stone from the middle of the dry river bed and stack them up on a spot inside their new camp. You see, God had told them ahead of time that He was going to perform this miracle to assure them that He was with them and would continue to be by their side as they fought off their enemies and possessed their new land. It was a lesson He did not want them to ever forget, and He wanted it to continue to impact subsequent generations.

As Christians, we are on a journey to a "promised land," as well. This life is to be a time of learning, growing, and reaching out to others. The Bible tells us we are being gradually conformed to the image of Christ Himself. Obviously, a major transformation is needed. Sometimes we cooperate with the process, sometimes we don't. God is going to do whatever it takes to keep us on the road, but the rate of speed is up to us.

Look at your life. Are you beginning the journey? Then you have some great adventures ahead of you. Seek God's face and you will see the signposts along the way. God will speak to you through the Scriptures, and you can speak with Him in prayer. But don't stop there. Look for His working in your life experiences. Have you been on the journey a long time? Then look back at the key moments in your life. What was God telling you? How did you respond? You see, God is a real person, and the Christian walk is a meaningful relationship with that Person. It is not just a set of religious beliefs or ecclesiastical traditions. And don't forget the lessons learned.

One of the presidents of the Christian college I attended had the students pile up some rocks at a special place on campus to memorialize a great event in the history of the college. He was patterning this after the story we looked at in the Book of Joshua. The pile of rocks would be a continual reminder of God's working. You may not want to pile up some rocks, but how about finding some other way to remind yourself of God's working in your life? Keep a journal. Post some mementos on your refrigerator or bulletin board. Keep some kind of record of it in a file or notebook labeled "Signposts." Whatever works for you. Whatever it takes to remember the lessons learned.

Chapter 19

SOME TIPS FOR THE JOURNEY

IF YOU WANT to see your divine signposts on life's journey, there are some things that you can do to help keep your eyes open along the way. Let me share with you some that I have found helpful:

Be sure to set aside some "alone time"

Obviously for the Christian, frequent time alone with God is vital. This requires time to meditate on the Scriptures so that God can speak to you and time in prayer speaking openly to Him in response. After all, any good relationship requires two-way communication. But I would also recommend an added dimension to your alone time. Include in your schedule what I call "think time." This is time to look carefully at your life. Time to evaluate where you are at (A bit of ruthless self-examination may be needed). I have found that this can be assisted by a long walk in the country or a stroll in your favorite park, and it can help you regain perspective lost in the hustle and bustle of everyday life.

By the way, I think this has almost become a lost art in our culture. Many people are too busy in business and family pursuits to find time to be alone. Others can hardly stand the thought of being alone. I have known people who even seem to go into a panic if their spouse is away or their friends are unavailable. Obviously, I am not advocating that you become some kind of hermit, but a balance is needed here. In the Gospels, even Jesus is seen to go off to a solitary place from time to time to get away from the crowds. It was undoubtedly a bigger challenge for Him than for any of us!

Learn to enjoy the simple things

When was the last time you stopped to smell a flower or watch a beautiful sunset? How often do you enjoy a good book while nestled in front of a nice fire in the fireplace with your dog curled up at your feet? Does the crystalline snow falling from the sky in winter still enchant you? Do you gaze at distant mountains with a longing in your heart? How often do you truly enjoy each bite of a meal you eat with a thankful heart?

You see, we take so many things for granted. We lose sight of many of the simple things in life that really give us joy. I remember as a child how fascinated I was watching a colony of ants do its thing. As an adult, the only time I even notice them is when they invade my house and I am forced to exterminate them. And yet Solomon, the wisest man to ever walk the face of the earth (except for Jesus, of course) tells us in the Book of Proverbs to observe the ants to learn what it means to be industrious and not lazy. My kids tease me because I "putter" in the yard so much, but I enjoy watching things grow and keeping an immaculate lawn and landscaping (I gave up the big garden a long time ago). It is a simple pleasure.

I attended all the Boise State home football games with my son while he was growing up. It was our special bonding time because we both love sports. I will never forget the time we were strolling through the campus on the way to a game and my son said to me, "Dad, we are making good memories that someday we will look back at." And he was right. We still talk about those times. More valuable than the many victories of the team on the field was the time we spent together.

Another special memory of a simple thing was the time my oldest daughter and I took a long bike ride together and found a place that had a vending machine with Squirt soda in it. She had never even heard of it, but I enjoyed it when I was growing up and introduced it to her. From that time on, we would always stop at the same place when riding our bikes, sit, and enjoy a Squirt together. We still reminisce about it from time to time.

I mentioned before that I used to be an avid runner. My youngest daughter became a bit of a fitness buff in high school, and we began doing some runs together. Those were special times to share a common interest and to talk about life together. It was certainly never time wasted.

When I was working swing shifts, my wife and I developed the habit of going out for brunch every Saturday. Since she was working day shifts, it was our time to catch up on each other's week and see how things had been going. It was important because we saw little of each other on week days. We enjoyed it so much that we still continue the habit even now that I am retired.

I could go on and on, but you get the point. Very often the best things are the simple things. Never forget that.

Never pass up a lemonade stand

We have all seen them. The little lemonade stands in summer manned by kids along the roadside. It is so easy to just drive by them, but I have tried to make it my policy to never pass them up. I stop and get a lemonade. Do you know why? Because even though I usually have no desire for a lemonade, especially when it is from an instant mix of some kind, I know how much it means to those kids. So many people pass them up that they are always thrilled when you give them some business. Not to mention they are learning an important life lesson about earning money for themselves.

What I am really saying is we need to make it a habit to do little acts of kindness toward others. It may mean just giving someone a smile or picking something up they have dropped. It may mean paying the difference for someone when they realize they don't quite have enough money for their groceries. Or how about giving someone a compliment? Sometimes the only time we voice all the nice things we appreciate about someone is at their funeral. If you are thinking something positive about someone, how about saying it to them while they are still alive? It can give them great encouragement. It might even make their day.

Let me give you a couple of examples of how much difference a kind word can make. I still remember when my high school sociology teacher took the time to tell each student something positive he had observed about them. When he came to me he said, "Dave, you have an uncanny ability in class discussions to sense what others are thinking and know just how to respond to them." As an insecure teenager, this did so much to boost my self-image. Similarly, I will never forget when the president of the college I attended caught me after a school function and said, "I am so proud of you as a student and how you have represented this college. I expect great things from you in the future." Those words meant a lot to me, and I have always felt a responsibility to honor them in my life. You see, taking a moment to say a few encouraging words can be a life-changing moment in someone's life.

You may say to me, "These are all little things. What about the big things we can do for people?" Without doubt, there will be opportunities to do some great things for others in your life. Be sure to be willing to do those things even when they require a great deal of personal sacrifice. You will never regret it. I am convinced that if we are not in the habit of doing the little things for others, we will be much less likely to do the more difficult ones. It's just the way things work.

Value people, not things

When Jesus was asked what was most important in life, He said that the two most important things were loving God and loving people (in that order). The apostle John in his first epistle made it clear that those two things are inseparable. You can't truly love God and not love people. I don't think many people come to the end of their life and wish that they had more things, but many people regret broken relationships. I know that when I look back at my life, I never feel bad about the things I didn't buy, but I do feel bad about missed opportunities to help people. It has also been said that there are only two things in this life that last forever, God's Word and people. I believe that is true; therefore, we should highly value both.

We have probably all known people who are materialists. They are in love with the things they possess and let you know it, and they usually look down on you if you have less. I remember when I was young and starting out in full-time ministry that the pay wasn't much, and my wife and I had very little in terms of furnishings for our first home. Most of what we had was used furniture passed down from our parents. Our only TV was a thirteen-inch black and white TV that had to be put on a plant stand because I couldn't afford an entertainment center. We had a church gathering in our home and one of the church members saw fit to make fun of the fact that we didn't even have a color TV. The funny thing is, that particular person had rarely shown a loving attitude toward other people and was never very supportive of us. In fact, he always seemed unhappy. I realized at that moment that I would never trade the material sacrifices we were called upon to make for the things that this man had and the life that he lived. I can't stress enough how important it is to keep your priorities straight.

Keep your eyes on eternity

We all know that the things of this life don't last. Everything wears out. Our clothes, our car, our bodies. That which is physical is temporary. Only that which is spiritual lasts forever. Clearly, then, the spiritual dimension of our lives should be our primary focus, but maintaining an eternal perspective is very difficult. I struggle with it every day. As physical beings, we tend to only think about those things that we can perceive with our senses. Yet the Scriptures tell us that faith is being convinced of things that are not seen (see Hebrews 11:1). We are told to fix our eyes on Jesus, even though He is physically no longer here (see Hebrews 12:2). And to cap it all off, we are told not to focus on the things which are seen because they are temporary, but rather to focus on those things that are unseen because they are eternal (see 2 Corinthians 4:18).

I believe there are two perspectives that help with this. One is to view the physical things of this life as "on loan" from God. If the ultimate ownership is God's, then He can do with it as He sees fit. For example, when the car you drive breaks down, instead of getting upset and frustrated about it, think of it as God's car. Realize that it is ultimately under His control and if He has allowed it to break down, it is for a good reason. Maybe He is teaching you patience. Maybe He is teaching you to trust Him for a solution. Ask for His wisdom and help instead of getting ticked off that your precious possession is damaged goods.

The other perspective is to always remember the big picture in life. Are you frustrated that you are being treated unfairly? Are you disturbed that society seems to be going to pot? Realize that it is all temporary. A day is coming when the King who judges righteously will return and set everything right. He is already preparing His mount to head into battle against evil. We are, in fact, told that we will one day view the troubles of this life as light and momentary when compared to the eternal glory that will be ours (see 2 Corinthians 4:17). Our flawed physical bodies will be transformed into new ones so full of splendor that if we saw such a being now, we would probably be inclined to fall prostrate before it. And that is only one part of the future redemption of the entire physical universe that we are told we can look forward to. With these things in mind, we will surely be far less myopic in the way we view life. Many things that have seemed so important to us will fade into insignificance in the light of such future glory.

Chapter 20

LEAVING A POSITIVE LEGACY

*The wise shall inherit glory,
But shame shall be the legacy of fools.
(Proverbs 3:35 NKJV)*

LIFE IS SHORT. In the Bible, it is compared variously to a mere breath (Psalm 39:5), to a morning mist that quickly vanishes (James 4:14), and to the grass that springs up and then quickly withers away (Psalm 103:15,16). This isn't intended to discourage us, but to remind us that our time on this earth is limited. We must make good use of it. There is nothing sadder than someone who comes to the end of their life and have little to show for it except a litany of regrets. I have been to more than one funeral where an individual was spoken of in glowing terms and those of us who knew him well thought to ourselves, "I must be at the wrong funeral, because I remember him as a mean and nasty old guy who never treated people well." Perhaps we missed something along the way, but what a sorry legacy to leave behind! I will never forget another funeral where I was asked to officiate. When I met with the son of the deceased to plan the service, he told me not to eulogize his mom because she was a wicked woman and he had nothing good to say about her. How terribly sad!

Legacy. What an important concept. It is what you leave behind when your life comes to an end. None of us are perfect. I have heard people look back on their lives and say they have no regrets, that they wouldn't change a thing. All I can say in response to that is that they must have been far too easy on themselves. At various times, we have all surely hurt others or failed to live up to our full potential. Even the Apostle Paul looked back with deep regret at how he had treated Christians before his conversion, but with God's help, we can all leave a positive legacy to impact generations to come. King David in the Old Testament had some major failings (like the terrible scandal with Bathsheba), but when God summed up David's life after he had passed from the scene, He described him as a man who had been fully devoted to God. Such is the nature of God's grace and forgiveness.

Let me share with you how God described some other people who left behind a positive legacy:

Enoch walked with God (Genesis 5:24).

Noah found favor in God's eyes because he was a righteous man (Genesis 6:8-9).

Abraham was called God's friend (James 2:23).

Moses was more humble than anyone else (Numbers 12:3).

John the Baptist was the greatest of all the prophets (Matthew 11:11).

The Apostle John was the disciple Jesus especially loved, apparently indicating that he was Jesus's closest friend (John 13:23).

So, here is the key question to ask yourself: When your life is over, what will be your legacy? How will others sum up your life?

Chapter 21

ENDING THE JOURNEY WELL

Surely goodness and love will follow me all the days of my life, and I will dwell in the house of the LORD forever. (Psalm 23:6 NIV)

MAYBE IT SOUNDS a bit morbid for me to talk more about the end of life's road. People often avoid any discussion about the final days of their lives. This is not surprising. It has been said that death is an obscenity foisted upon us by the Fall. I agree. It was not God's original intention for mankind. In a sense, it is the most unnatural thing we can imagine. Evolutionists try to tell us that it is just a normal event in the cycle of life and a necessary part of the survival of the fittest, but if you believe in God and supernatural creation, you believe that the actual cause is sin, and therefore, things are not right in this world. If you are a Christian, you also believe that in the end, the death and resurrection of Christ will make everything right again. For the one who believes in Him, even death is an ushering into a better existence beyond this life; an eternity that includes a restoration of Paradise and everything that God intended in Eden (and more). In the meantime, we must make the best of our days and seek to end our journey well.

Ending well involves a number of things. One is making sure that relationships that have been damaged be mended whenever possible. It would be sad to leave this life with a rift remaining between you and another human being. Have you noticed how that as people get to the later years of life they have a tendency to look back at times when they feel they may have hurt someone and wish they could go back and change things or, at the very least, have had the opportunity to apologize? Often the people involved are long gone from their lives. I recently apologized to someone for something I thought was hurtful that I said many years ago when we were both young. The person I thought I had offended said that she didn't even remember the incident I referred to and certainly was not deeply hurt, but you know what? The confession was good for me. I did not want to go to the grave having this thing on my conscience.

Another thing we should consider is whether or not we have some unfinished goals we have set for ourselves. With the freedom that comes with retirement, for example, you can devote yourself more fully to something you have always wanted to do, but didn't have the time. Obviously, some of those may be things like traveling to places we have never gone or spending more time with the grandkids, but it should not be limited to that. For me, it was doing more writing, hence this book.

Most importantly, stay true to yourself and the God you serve until the very end. At the end of his life, the Apostle Paul was able to say that he had "finished the course" (his life journey) and "kept the faith." Too often in their senior years people become disheartened and bitter because of the difficulty of changing life circumstances and the inevitable physical decline that comes with aging. This can be very destructive and even cause some to turn away from God altogether. Don't let that happen to you! The Bible tells us that although our bodies are gradually wasting away, we are being spiritually renewed day by day (2 Corinthians 4:16).

Let me finish with this. A full lifespan can be compared to the seasons of the year. Youth is like spring, early adulthood like summer, adulthood past one's prime like autumn, and the senior years like winter. Each season of life has its own beauty, but no one would choose perpetual winter. We always look eagerly forward to spring and the new life it brings. That it is why it is so important that by faith we can also look forward to the promise of a new spring at the end of the world; a perfect existence

where the birds sing, the sparkling waters flow, where dreams are fulfilled, and familiar faces greet us with open arms. The new Jerusalem where signposts are no longer needed. A blessedly new heaven and earth greater than our most hopeful imaginings. You see, for the Christian, the journey has just begun. I love the way that C.S. Lewis portrays the end of this life and the beginning of the next at the end of *The Chronicles of Narnia* as he describes the children's destiny: "All their life in this world and all their adventures in Narnia had only been the cover and the title page: now at last they were beginning Chapter One of the Great Story which no one on earth has read: which goes on for ever: in which every chapter is better than the one before."[3] Without doubt, the best is yet to come.

---

[3] C.S. Lewis, *The Last Battle* (Great Britain: HarperCollins, 2014), 222.

POSTSCRIPT

I WOULD BE REMISS to not add one more personal note. Perhaps your life has been a struggle and you feel that you have not handled your journey well. Don't give up. God will never give up on you. One of my favorite quotes is "God is easy to please, but hard to satisfy" (George MacDonald, as quoted by C.S. Lewis).[4] In other words, He will settle for nothing less than His best path for you, but He is excited for every baby step you take along the way.

While writing this book, I was diagnosed with an aggressive cancer. At this point, after surgery, several subsequent tests have shown no remaining cancer. This was an amazing answer to prayer and a special blessing from God, but it is not a guarantee that there are no cancer cells still in my body. My future is in God's hands and that is what really matters. The same is true for you. My cancer has been an important reminder, perhaps even a signpost, to me that life brings many unexpected twists and turns, and many walk a more difficult road than I do. It is far more important how we respond to the difficult times than that we fully understand why they come our way.

My hope and prayer for you is that you will always listen for God's gentle, quiet voice in every situation. He loves you and wants to speak His love into your life just as He has so often spoken it into mine.

---

[4] C.S. Lewis, *Mere Christianity,* 1997 Book of the Month Club edition (by arrangement with Scribner, a division of Simon & Schuster, Inc.), 158.

www.ingramcontent.com/pod-product-compliance
Ingram Content Group UK Ltd.
Pitfield, Milton Keynes, MK11 3LW, UK
UKHW041949230426
12048UKWH00008B/229